Lost
in an
Adult
Community

Finding God in the wilderness

God Bless ♥

M.B. ROOSA

MBR

Lost in an Adult Community - Finding God in the wilderness - by M.B. Roosa

ISBN 978-0-578-32706-8

Cover Design & Illustration by James Koenig - www.freelancefridge.com

"This book is dedicated to my mother, Esther Stout. Her love for the Lord, prayer, and the body of Christ was infectious, not only to me, but to countless others who had the privilege of knowing her. Even when I wasn't particularly funny, she laughed at my jokes. I miss you, Mom!"

- M.B. Roosa -

INTRODUCTION

When my parents were alive, they lived in an adult community. They never joined in on Bingo night or tennis tournaments. They never played shuffleboard, nor did they even have block parties. They simply enjoyed the peace and quiet of a neighborhood full of their peers. Their only qualm was that eventually their neighbors started going away and I am not talking about vacationing in Bora Bora. They had to witness many nice neighbors go home to meet their Maker. Not only was it sad to say goodbye, but it caused my parents the shocking realization of their own mortality. Something a lively senior does not want to think about on a daily basis.

That is why I had the goal of never moving into one of these communities. I guess in my mind the thought of being in a neighborhood still buzzing with young folk (yes, I called them folk) would make me feel more alive. But then it happened. My kids grew up and moved out and the silence was like an angelic symphony to my ears.

Now, perhaps, if we had only one child or even two children leaving the home, I would have more readily felt the pangs of remorse of an empty nest. But because seven kids were gone, seven loud active happy stop-looking-out-my-window kids, I no longer had to find my peace and quiet within the privacy of the commode. After a few years of enjoying the new repose, we decided it was time to downsize.

Welcome to my story.

PROLOGUE

It was the beginning of 2017 when our new house was almost ready for move in. We were excited for the upcoming adventure into senior land until my husband discovered some flaws in our new build. Being a former licensed contractor who put hard work and quality into everything he built, it was a disappointment, to say the least. There was actually a serious moment in time when we considered backing out of the contract, and I can't help wondering what would have happened if we had.

For one thing, my husband would have never discovered pickleball. I mean what would the man have done for all those two-hour time slots three times a week if he couldn't spend it slamming a plastic ball across a net? Nor would he have discovered that going to the community gym early in the morning to work his biceps was a good time to exercise without a lot of company.

While I (the introvert) sat at home and tried to figure out what to do with my life sans a giant home and three years of purging and packing, my husband (the extrovert) hopped right into his new role and met every Don, Mick, and Gary in our neighborhood.

But all was not lost on me. There have been a couple of benefits for me moving here as well. Not only have I met some genuinely nice people, but I also have unlimited and hilarious material to work with. So, for this introvert who is also a writer, what can be better than that?

Most importantly, I have learned some lessons about walking with God through the wildernesses of life.

1

Job 15:10 (NAS) "Both the gray-haired and the
aged are among us...."

You aren't kidding, folks!

It is April. *"Must have been that left turn in
Albuquerque,"* said Bugs Bunny and me. In my
quest for the community mailbox in my
neighborhood where I had been living for over
a year, I forgot to go straight down the main
thoroughfare and so I decided to meander
through side streets rather than making a U-
turn on the main road and possibly knocking a
couple of octogenarians off their tricycles.

I am not intending to be rude. Some of my
neighbor's tricycles are state of the art, with

every bell and whistle you can imagine. Some are even motorized. I am also not trying to be disrespectful for those in a higher age bracket, because quite frankly, I have discovered that most of them are in better shape than I am.

Now being the introvert that I am and not joining the pickle ball club, water aerobics, or embarrassing myself on a yoga mat, (been there) I hadn't ventured through the neighborhood, so this was all new territory. I passed houses I'd never seen before (which didn't really matter because they pretty much all look alike) and a plethora of attached condos that butt up against the golf course. Of course, there were lots of golf carts (I can't emphasize this enough) driven by the majority of seniors who have never set foot on a golf course.

When are you going to get your golf cart? I'm not. I have a car. Also, I would rather spend the $3,000 on 120 outfits at *Ross*. Thank you.

I drove by men in large brim hats, Bermuda shorts, and high white socks. I even waved to a couple of walkers who wore visors advertising the community. My visor is currently hiding somewhere in my closet with the windbreaker vest they gave me during the closing of our property.

There were dollar store flowers popping out of colorful pots by front doors, lots of American flags blowing in the breeze, and shiny Corvettes tucked away in garages mostly for bragging rights or the occasional car show. This is my life. Although the people are friendly, I have to wonder when, in the world, did I grow old enough to live here?

Perhaps, I thought, this would be a good time to ask God what he wanted to do with me here.

There are many seasons in life we must travel through. Some are exciting, like the anticipation of a wedding or a new baby. Others are heartbreaking and emotionally trying, like the loss of a dream, a serious illness, or the death of someone we love. Within these seasons it is imperative that we know that God walks with us through each one. He is always available to rejoice with us, encourage us to keep going, and He will even carry us when we are unable to move forward.

The older I become the more I have experienced and understand this truth. And even though I am in the Autumn of my life (and probably much closer to Winter than I am willing to admit), I know that I know that He will always be with me.

The Bible puts it this way:

"Do not fear, for I am with you; do not anxiously look about you, for I am your God. I will strengthen you, surely, I will help you. Surely I will uphold you with My righteous right hand." Isaiah 41:10 (NAS)

2

Genesis 16:7 (NAS) "Now the angel of the Lord found her (Hagar) by a spring of water in the wilderness…"

Apparently, she lived in an Arizona adult community.

It was May. Snowbirds had flown home. Streets were as empty as an Arizona ghost town in the 60s. Hot wind blew from the west, whipping my hair around, whistling past my ears. Walking to the mailbox was like high noon in a spaghetti western. (If you don't know what a spaghetti western is, ask your Nana) The only thing missing was a tumbleweed rolling across my path.

And of course, Clint Eastwood.

Although I was not cast out of my former home like poor Hagar, it has been during times of loneliness and emptiness, when I felt like a castaway, that God used my circumstance to draw me closer to Him.

The first two summers in our new community felt like wilderness for me. My husband was finding his place, meeting neighbors, building friendships, while I had only spoken to one or two couples. I am sure being an introvert was part of my problem. It has oftentimes been the bane of my existence and has hindered me from stepping out in faith and moving forward.

I knew God brought us here. At least I hoped that we had heard from Him when making our decision to downsize. But I certainly wasn't feeling quite at home as I had anticipated. So, that is when I began to pray and ask the Lord to direct my steps. To give me direction. To help me find my place in this adult community.

But let me tell you, it did not happen right away.

Just like Hagar, I felt alone. Dejected even. Until God revealed to me a spring of water in the desert in the form of a writer's club. It had been there all along. I hadn't seen what was right in front of me because, quite frankly, I didn't look. However, it would soon become the place where I could go and be myself. Where I could meet friends, all of whom love God, and have a similar focus on life. I had finally found my haven, my oasis in a desert place. I only had to open my eyes. I give God all the glory!

Do you ever feel like you are in a dry empty place and could use your own oasis? Trust God. He loves you! He knows your needs. He already has a place for you. It is right around the corner.

"And the Lord will continually guide you, and satisfy your desire in scorched places, and give strength to your bones: and you will be like a watered garden, and like a spring of water whose waters do not fail." Isaiah 58:11 (NAS)

3

1 Corinthians 9:27 (NAS) "…but I buffet my body and make it my slave, lest possibly, after I have preached to others, I myself should be disqualified."

Buffet, as in afflict or harm repeatedly!

The gym. The free, conveniently located chamber of humiliation brought to you by our local HOA. As soon as I enter the below zero exercise facility I am accosted by mirrors. Everywhere I turn they seem to be yelling at me: "What on earth happened to your thirty-year-old-Jane-Fonda-feel-the-burn-tape-obsessed-body?"

I lower my head in shame and move to a

machine where I am guaranteed legs like Carrie Underwood. But alas, there sits Miss-stick-figure-Jones. She literally sits - resting for ten long minutes between 5 short reps. What is she waiting for? The Publishers Clearing House van to arrive with a bouquet of flowers and a giant check? If I weren't a Christian woman, I would tell her to get off my machine and go eat a bowl of ice cream. I mean can't she see I'm waiting? Can't she see I need the machine more than she does?

Instead, I hold my tongue and move to an exercise bike and begin pedaling. Afterall, my body is a temple that I need to maintain. Right? I am panting, heart rate 120, bored to tears, longest mile, and a half of my life. I stop, catch my breath, and look at the screen. I've burned 4 calories.

Will I return? Of course, I will. I don't think Jane Fonda makes exercise videos anymore.

At my age working out has become a necessity rather than a desire to look like a super model. Trust me, that ship has not only sailed, but is taking on water. Of course, I would like to look my best for my age. I mean, who wouldn't? But let's get real here. I have given birth to five babies and have been fighting gravity for over sixty years. Trust me. There's not enough *Botox* on earth to help this girl.

The ugly truth is that this temple is not the same as when it was young. My dad in his later years, who was the funniest guy on the planet, would often say when rising from his seat at the dinner table, "this is the chair that rigor mortis set in." It cracked me up every single time he said it. But now that I am older, it is more true than funny.

The Lord recently put this question on my heart: "What in this life drives you?" Is it pride? Is it self-esteem? Is it making money or fulfilling the dreams I had to lay aside to take care of my family? Or is my drive to be led completely and utterly by the will of God and His word?

I don't know how long I have left on earth. I do know where I am going and sometimes as I look to the clouds, I definitely feel a longing like nothing else. But until that day arrives, I want His will in my life. I want to have the strength to draw closer and closer to Him every day. I want to be a healthy vessel that is so full of His love that it overflows to those around me. I want my drive to be Him alone.

I will be the first to admit that I have a long way to go. And if you are being honest, you will admit that you do too. But in the meantime, we must do our best to lay what we lack at the foot of the cross and trust our Creator with the progress. Nothing good can be accomplished without first yielding to the One who not only loves us, but who created every fiber of our being.

"But seek first His kingdom and His righteousness; and all these things shall be added to you." Matthew 6:33 (NAS)

4

Genesis 3:19b(NAS) "…For you are dust, and to dust you shall return."

This is especially true during monsoon season.

As I have mentioned before, if you would have asked me twenty years ago if I would ever move into an adult community, I would have answered with a resounding "no way!" I was also passionately opposed to any neighborhood where all of the houses not only looked alike but were also all adorned in dirt-colored paint.

The enormity of our decision to move to such a neighborhood hit me square in the face during our last dust storm. Literally. I was outside. When the dirt cloud rolled in from the south all the houses on my block disappeared. And unfortunately, there aren't enough *Swiffer Dusters* in the world to solve the problem.

But then again, there really are many benefits to living in an adult community: A heated pool in the summer, a freezing gym in the winter, and the many genuinely nice neighbors – most of which are named Mary, Gary, or Donald.

Apparently, parents in the 40s and 50s were not as creative in choosing names for their children. You could go door to door in my community and never find a person named Coco, Apple, or Chocolate. You may find a Brandy, Sherry, or Chardonnay – but that would be in the wine glass they carry when going to get their mail.

Moving into an adult community in the middle of the Arizona desert has definitely at times felt like a walk in the wilderness – both physically and spiritually. It has definitely been an adjustment.

Regardless of where we are in this amazing life God has given us, there will also be hardships, trials, and pain. I, like you, have had my share of all these things. But I have found that it is because of hardships, trials, and pain that I lean more often into my relationship with the Lord.

I read a beautiful book about a woman in the midst of a horrifying war who went through devastation like we have not seen in this nation. And yet at the same time when her children were weary of praying, she admonished them with words like these, "be thankful we have a reason to pray."

What a powerful statement! If everything in our lives were perfect, perhaps we would not be as compelled to pray, to seek God, to come before Him as often and ask for His help. God does not desire for us to be in pain. He loves to heal us, to bring us victory. That's why He sent His son to die on the cross. But God does desire our prayers. He longs for the sweet fellowship of spending time with us. He loves it when we call Him Abba Father and ask for His help. I want nothing more than to be close to my Savior. And the wonderful thing about it, is that He promises that when we call on Him, He will meet us there.

"Many are the afflictions of the righteous; But the Lord delivers him out of them all." Psalms 34:19 (NAS)

5

Galatians 5:22 (NAS) "But the fruit of the
Spirit is love, joy, peace, patience…"

*"Patience is a virtue, possess it if you can.
Seldom found in women. Never found in man."*

They say patience is a virtue. If that's true, then
today I had no virtue at all.

Due to heavy construction on the road I
usually take to get out of my neighborhood, I
once again found myself meandering through
residential streets to reach my destination. In
front of me was a person driving so slowly (as
my father always put it) you'd have to set
stakes to see if he were moving at all. Now
evidently nobody had ever told this poor driver

that he had a rearview mirror, because no amount of flailing my arms got his attention or caused him to speed up or pull over.

I would have honked my horn, but in this neighborhood, one must be sensitive to heart conditions and other such ailments. I certainly didn't need that on my conscience. So, there I was - stuck. I mean we were going so slowly a desert tortoise passed us on the sidewalk.

When I finally couldn't take it anymore, I revved the engine, and whipped around the vehicle at a whopping 15 miles an hour and left him eating my dust. That was hours ago. But I can't help wondering if that driver is still making his way home.

Luke 12: 25 (NASV) "And which of you by being anxious can add a single cubit to his life's span."

Well, apparently not me.

Patience, I have to admit, is definitely lacking in my character. Granted, I am better at waiting than I was maybe twenty years ago, but still, it is a struggle. With impatience comes the inevitable anxiety. And we all know that anxiety can bring on health issues (or, in my case, an addiction to snacking).

Anxiety is so prevalent in our society today.

Of course, with the day's current events such as the pandemic, violence, riots, abortion, and human trafficking there is a very real reason to deal with fear. Sin is amplified on the news. It is almost glorified on some networks. And if you are like me, you are praying things go back to normal. Whatever that is.

But let me share what I genuinely believe is happening here. I believe it is satan's last stand, and even though we know God wins in the end and there is victory for us today in Jesus, it is an ugly world out there.

But in the midst of all of this turmoil I often wonder how I, as a child of God could even allow impatience, fear, depression, and anxiety to overtake the peace that He so willingly offers?

If you are like me, you are impatient for peace. You crave peace. You want to feel secure in your home. You want to know your children and grandchildren are free from harm and danger. You want the Lord to surround you, your family, and your friends every minute of every hour of every day. Here's the good news - He does. He is fighting a spiritual battle on our behalf; a battle we cannot see with our human eyes. Our job is to simply pray, believe, and to give thanks that He has everything under control.

This is not an easy accomplishment. But as we learn to keep our eyes on the Victor, no matter what is going on around us, He will enable us to experience a peace that defies all odds.

Philippians 4:6-7 (NAS) "Be anxious for nothing, but in everything by prayer and supplication with thanksgiving let your requests be made known to God. And the peace of God, which surpasses all comprehension, will guard your hearts and your minds in Christ Jesus."

6

1 Timothy 5:13 (NAS) "At the same time they also learn to be idle, as they go around from house to house; and not merely idle, but also gossips and busybodies, talking about things not proper to mention."

Apparently retire is synonymous with inquire.

I am thankful that I am an introvert. Because what I hear from my husband is that gossip flows quite freely in our community. I mean there is more backbiting in this neighborhood than at a mosquito-infested nudist camp. It's like high school all over again and I once again find myself playing it as incognito as possible.

If I'm not outside my neighborhood hanging

with grandkids, grocery shopping, or antique shopping (what I now call shopping for clothes), then I am most likely inside my house writing, reading, cleaning, cooking, or watching reruns of my favorite Hallmark movie. I have a few acquaintances in the neighborhood to whom I will have a short chat (mostly about what parts of our bodies are aching this week), but I seriously cannot get caught up in all the neighborhood gossip. I can't.

(I can listen to it. But I would never repeat it.)

I have to say that in my new community there is no lack of things to talk about. Apparently, there are quite a number of people who simply have nothing else to do with their lives, sans work and children, then to talk about their neighbors. I have heard all kinds of stories – ones you would never hear in a neighborhood full of young people because quite frankly we have apparently landed on another planet. At least that's how it feels to me sometimes. And it's amazing how much one can glean about certain residents if one were to simply stand there and listen. It can definitely make for great comedy material. But it can also shed the wrong light on the person who is the subject of the chatter.

God is not pleased with any form of gossip or backbiting. According to His Word the very morsel of gossip can separate the most intimate of friends and can only cause strife.

Proverbs 20:19 (NAS) "He who goes about as a slanderer reveals secrets. Therefore, do not associate with a gossip."

As humans we are all going to be confronted with gossip now and then. If we are being honest, we are like magnets to a juicy story. I know I am guilty of this. And it takes a lot of self-control not to repeat something about a certain person that is not only shocking, but hilarious at the same time.

But as a child of God, I desire to do His will. And His will is for us to be prudent and not speak ill of others. So, I find I must be on my guard at all times from being easily sucked into the vortex of juicy gossip about others and ask the Lord for forgiveness when I mess up.

1 Timothy 3:11 (NAS) "Women must likewise be dignified, not malicious gossips, but temperate, faithful in all things."

7

Psalms 48:14 (NAS) "For such is God, our God forever and ever; He will guide us until death."

Until death? This is good news!

I recently did a search of all the activities available here in our adult community, and let me say, there is quite a selection. Here are some examples:

1. Chair aerobics. This is something I would never attempt to do. For one thing, I have a fear of heights.

2. Chair yoga. Sounded interesting. But if one tried downward dog on a chair, wouldn't one

slide off onto one's face?

3. Block watch. That sounds completely boring. I'd rather watch TV.

4. Corvette Club. I tried to join that one, but evidently you have to have a Corvette. La-di-da!

5. Scuba & Snorkeling. Now come on. What do they think they're going to find on the bottom of the community pool?

6. Tennis club. I used to play tennis. But with a racket, not a club.

Life, like my new community, can be full of choices. Some of them will enrich our lives, and some simply fill our lives with unnecessary busyness. It's okay to get out there and have fun and meet new people. However, there can often be a fine line between doing everything available to us and praying that God guides us and helps us fill our time wisely. But what is the balance?

I am reminded of the story in Luke chapter 10 when Jesus was traveling, and Martha invited Him into her home. It is obvious that Martha's intentions were pure. She only wanted to serve the Lord and hospitality was obviously one of her giftings. But the problem with

Martha was she became so distracted with all the things she was doing that she forgot whom she was serving. And when her sister Mary took a break to sit at Jesus' feet, Martha became angry. But she didn't just get angry at her sister, she also became frustrated with Jesus.

Luke 10:40 (NAS) "...Lord, do You not care that my sister has left me to do all the serving alone? Then tell her to help me."

I have to say, that took chutzpah for Martha to speak to Jesus that way. And yet are we any different than Martha? Do we fill our lives with so many things, that we forget whom we are serving? What did Jesus have to say about this?

Luke 10:41-42 (NAS) "But the Lord answered and said to her, "Martha, Martha, you are worried and bothered about so many things; but only a few things are necessary, really only one, for Mary has chosen the good part, which shall not be taken away from her."

So, my prayer is that before we begin anything new, whether it is for fun, exercise, or even for ministry, that we seek the Lord for guidance and we don't become so busy with life that we forget whom we are serving.

Colossians 3:23-24 (NAS) "Whatever you do, do your work heartily, as for the Lord rather than for men; knowing that from the Lord you will receive the reward of the inheritance. It is the Lord Christ whom you serve."

8

Ecclesiastes 3:4 (KJV) "A time to weep, and a time to laugh; a time to mourn, and a time to dance…"

Dance? What if someone is watching?

This may or may not have anything to do with living in an adult community. I seriously have no idea. But since we moved here, we have had a plethora of different mail carriers. Some of them are apparent veterans of the job driving up in their USPS van. While others, dressed in AZ casual have delivered our mail in their own personal vehicles. I have no qualms about how I get the mail, as long as the person delivering it is a professional mail carrier. However, I am not sure how to summarize this particular experience.

As I walked (well actually limped, I had tendonitis in my right ankle at the time) to retrieve our mail, I was accosted by loud jazz music. I mean REALLY loud jazz music. At first, I thought one of my octogenarian neighbors was having an afternoon dance-off, which I have to say wouldn't have surprised me in the least. But as I reached the corner, I realized the music was reverberating from a 4-door pick-up truck parked in front of our cluster mailbox.

As I crossed the street, I discovered a man wearing nylon gym shorts, t-shirt, and sneakers. His head was down between two metals doors and his rear-end was rocking back and forth to the music. I wasn't sure if he was delivering mail or if his head was stuck in a slot. I also wasn't sure what to do. Should I offer the man my assistance or go home and wash my eyes out with soap?

I decided to return home and simply wait to retrieve my mail until the music subsided and the dancer had departed.

The mail carrier probably had no idea I was watching, but I have to say it was quite amusing to see him moving with reckless abandon to the lively tune. Frankly, as I was watching him, I had to keep from tapping my foot as well.

The Bible says that David danced before the Lord with all his might. That must have been some powerful dancing! He was unabashed and unashamed to worship God with every fiber of his being.

I was raised Lutheran. And so, I was accustomed to entering the church quietly and sitting there piously listening to the Pastor preach. We sang, but never raised our hands and we most definitely never got out of the pew and danced.

I honestly believe there is a time to be reverent and humble. It is when we quiet our spirits before the Lord, that we can hear Him as He speaks to our hearts. But I also believe there is a time for rejoicing – when we lay down our inhibitions and worship the Lord with all our might. We certainly don't have a problem celebrating when our favorite baseball player hits a homerun, or our favored football team scores a touchdown, or even when our kids return to school after a long hot summer. Woohoo!

How much more worthy is our worship to our Lord and Savior who died on the cross for us so we could have eternal life? Now *that* is something to dance about!

Psalm 149:3 "Let them praise His name with dancing; Let them sing praises to Him with timbrel and lyre."

9

2 Corinthians 10:12 (NIV) "We do not dare to classify or compare ourselves with some who commend themselves. When they measure themselves by themselves and compare themselves with themselves, they are not wise."

Wait a minute. What?

The one thing about our neighborhood is that the majority of all the senior citizens who live here are searching for the fountain of youth. They swim, ride bike, play pickleball, play tennis, play baseball, work out in the gym, or go for jogs with the hope that by doing so somehow, they will avoid the inevitable. Not necessarily death, mind you, but definitely high blood pressure or triple bypass surgery. Some of them don themselves in matching Lycra and shiny Spandex exercise outfits, the kind of bright colors that can blind you on a moonless night. I know because I pass them on my daily walks.

Most of them, I have to say, are friendly and wave as you pass them by. But then there are some far too superior to greet a woman wearing worn Levi capris and her husband's Coca-Cola t-shirt, making me want to rush to our local Walmart for something more stylish.

But then there is the woman I passed a while ago. She greeted me with a "good morning" and a wave. She was not dressed in fancy *Under Armour* or *Nike* attire. She wasn't even wearing her husband's t-shirt. She was proud as a peacock marching down the asphalt bike lane dressed only in a button-down cotton house dress (a duster as mother used to call it), sneakers, and huge smile.

And I couldn't help thinking that she will probably outlive us all.

As humans we tend to judge ourselves and others by our outward appearance. I personally have struggled with roller coaster weight gain and loss my entire life. And I have actually had people judge me mercilessly.

When I was a kid, my next-door neighbor called me marshmallow. And no, I was not as wide as I was short. One of my friend's dad called me slim. I may have been a kid, but I wasn't dumb. And I knew this was his way of making a jab at my not so slender childhood physique. But I have to admit that most of the judgment against my person has been from the gal in the mirror. She has been tormenting me my entire life.

They say when you get older you quit caring. Well, that is not the case. But hopefully you become wiser. The lines on your face may not be aesthetically pleasing as your once youthful skin, but if you let them, they can remind you of all the joyful times you had with friends in the sun. The extra weight around the middle may be difficult to get rid of, but it can remind you of the wonderful children God has blessed you with.

I have an amazing friend named Effie. As of this writing she is 95 years young. I have been blessed to hear stories of her incredible life and family by her writings that she has shared at our writer's club. And even though she has physical limitations, she gets up every morning, gets dressed, puts on makeup, and does her hair. She is an utter delight to spend time with. But that is because Effie loves God and her inner beauty shines through her every single day. Effie has figured out life and is still living it to the best of her ability. And I have to say, I want to be like Effie when I grow up.

Let's face it. Growing older can be rough on the outward appearance. But with Jesus in our hearts and minds, His love will outshine any doubt that we are created in His image. And what can be better than that?

1 Samuel 16:7b (NAS) "God sees not as man sees, for man looks at the outward appearance, but the Lord looks at the heart."

10

1 Corinthians 9:24 (NAS) "Do you not know that those who run in a race all run, but only one receives the prize? Run in such a way that you may win."

I'll be lucky if I can limp to the finish line.

Except during the unbearably hot summers in Arizona, I like to get up early and walk as much as possible and try to get in at least 30 minutes of exercise before breakfast. This morning, for some reason, I found it such a chore to walk.

Our neighborhood has a slight incline when heading east and today I felt every muscle in my thighs as I was heading home. I wasn't out of breath; I was simply out of energy and wished with every pathetic step that I had stayed home in bed.

While I was trudging along, having my own personal pity-party, and seriously considering calling home to have my husband to come and get me, I looked up to see a lady walking along the sidewalk with the aid of a walker. She was probably going faster than I was and I was thankful we weren't headed the same direction, or she may have passed me. How humiliating would THAT be? So, I lifted my chin off the asphalt, pulled up my big girl britches, and made a beeline for home.

I had such high hopes for the new year. But didn't we all? 2020 was supposed to be a year of fulfilled dreams and goals, and everyone I know was anticipating great things. Then the pandemic hit which seemed to let loose every demon from hell and our nation suffered more than sickness and death. It's as if the devil himself opened up hell's gates and released evil like we haven't seen before in this nation. And those vulnerable to his ploys, put down their guards and moral dignity, and began attacking everyone and everything in sight. Many innocent, and hard-working Americans lost their businesses and even lives to senseless violence, and it has been difficult to understand why any of this had to happen.

My morning walk was simply a symbol of how the trials and evils of this life can zap us of our energy and in some cases cause us to want to give up entirely. But even in these dark days, God has never changed. He is still our Hope. He is still on His throne. And even though we can't see Him working with our physical eyes, trust me, He is working.

So, how can we survive evil days such as these? By spending time with the only One who can see the future and can keep us in the palm of His hand. He calmed the raging sea for His disciples. He fed the multitude with a young boy's lunch. He turned water into wine, and He raised the dead to life. But best of all, He is still the same God today. But then why all this chaos?

The Lord never promised us a life without trials. What He did promise was that when we passed through them it would produce in us good things.

James 1:2-4 (NAS) "Consider it all joy, my brethren, when you encounter various trials, knowing that the testing of your faith produces endurance. And let endurance have its perfect result, so that you may be perfect and complete, lacking in nothing."

Only the Lord can give us the strength and

grace to walk through dark times. If we look to Him to meet all of our needs, He will do it. I know He will give us the energy to keep moving forward no matter what life throws our way. Afterall, He is our example. Trust Him.

Hebrews 12:2a (NAS) "Fixing our eyes on Jesus, the author and perfecter of faith, who for the joy set before Him endured the cross…"

11

Proverbs 21:19 (NAS) "It is better to live in a desert land than with a contentious and vexing woman."

But what if living in the desert is WHY she is contentious??

Snails, quails, and cottontails chased by a coyote.

Thyroid pills, Epi-pens, medical peyote.

Walkers, joggers, Irish Cloggers, pickle-ballers, too.

Tennis players, chapel prayers, snowbirds passing through.

Softball bases, friendly faces, who could ask for more?

Crazy drivers crashing places, injuries galore.

Cholla cacti, tiger aloe, Bougainvillea vine,

Prickly pear, eagle claw, watered by canine.

Golf carts, golf carts, many golf carts, everywhere you turn.

Swimming, gymming, never grinning work out till you burn.

Senior living, no misgiving, brings joyfulness and sorrow.

Will I stay? Perhaps, today. But maybe not tomorrow.

© 2019 - M.B. Roosa

I wouldn't exactly call myself a contentious or vexing woman, but I have definitely had my share of grumpy days. I really don't know if it is due to the fact that I am old enough to be living in an adult community, or because after all these years I still dwell in a desert.

I was born in Ohio, you know, one of those states which has actual seasons. I had no vote into whether or not we moved to Arizona. At the age of three, I was too young to hire a lawyer or even create a protest sign demanding my right to choose. So, I was brought here with my family in a station wagon loaded with everything we owned and have never left. That part, I'll admit, is at least partially my own fault.

The Arizona desert only has one hot and one cool season, basically a brutally long and hot summer followed by a few months of mild winter. The cool weather never seems to last long enough. Just the other day I was excited because my weather app said the temperature was dropping for a day.

"It's only going to be 99 tomorrow!" I squealed with delight. To which my husband burst out laughing.

My only reprieve is when I get to visit family in Flagstaff. Although it is still in Arizona, it is in the mountains and has real, God-created seasons and fresh air. Thank the Lord for that!

Jesus experienced the wilderness in a much deeper way than any of us have. For one thing, he was fasting for forty days and forty nights and the devil himself came to tempt Him with bread and water. If I fasted for forty days and forty nights and the devil came to temp me, I would probably eat the devil.

All of us experience wilderness moments in our lives. Times of loneliness, discouragement, or devastation. There are moments when we feel stuck in a place without escape and depression inevitably joins the party. When Jesus went through His wilderness experience, He did not give in to his hunger, He did not give in to temptation, and He did not grumble or complain. He simply rebuked the devil and commanded him to hit the road.

The good news is that we too, as God's children, have authority over the enemy. We have the power to rebuke and bind him when he comes to torment us. So, no matter what wilderness we are currently in, instead of griping and grumbling and moaning over our circumstances, we can stand up to the enemy and tell him, like Jesus did, to hit the road.

Jesus put it this way:

Matthew 16:19 (NAS) "I will give you the keys of the kingdom of heaven; and whatever you shall bind on earth shall have been bound in heaven, and whatever you shall loose on earth shall have been loosed in heaven."

This is good news!

12

Hebrews 11:1 (KJV) "Now faith is the substance of things hoped for, the evidence of things not seen."

Open my spiritual eyes, Lord!

Have you ever seen the movie *I Am Legend*?

In the summer months they could use my neighborhood for a sequel. When the sun is highest in the sky and it's safe to go out, the streets are as empty as a politician's heart. Snowbirds have flown the coop and many other neighbors are on vacation which leaves an eerie cloud of emptiness and silence overhead. No newspapers in sight, window blinds closed to those who remain, and Roll-A-Shield shutters tighter than last year's jeans.

There may not be a Blockbuster in the neighborhood but there is definitely a mannequin watching from a window. I have also seen a German shepherd and a Shelby Mustang. The only part missing from this sequel is Will Smith.

In the movie Will Smith's character is alone in his world and we often hear him speaking to his dog or even a mannequin in his local video store. Personally, when I'm alone, I talk to myself. Which can be quite embarrassing when my husband enters the room.

However, the Bible makes it quite clear that we are never truly alone. God is always with us. I am certain that I am not the only one who has faced times of loneliness where I feel like even God has abandoned me. It is like my prayers hit the ceiling and His presence seems nowhere to be found. But because He has promised to never leave us or forsake us, that is the time when our faith in Him and His word becomes the "substance" of that promise. It's the time to trust Him and stand on His word. And as we worship Him for His goodness to us, it won't be long before His presence will flow over us like precious anointing oil.

So, when loneliness and emptiness tries to

take over your spirit, always remember that God is omnipresent (present everywhere at the same time). And even when we do not feel Him, He is there. All we have to do is rest in that assurance. Stand on His word. Worship Him anyway. Thank Him for always being there, even when we feel lonely.

James 4:8a (NKJV) "Draw near to God and He will draw near to you."

13

Romans 12:4-5 (NIV) "For just as each of us has one body with many members, and these members do not all have the same function, so in Christ we, though many, form one body, and each member belongs to all the others."

Do you ever feel like you're the hang nail in the body of Christ?

I used to play racquetball. I used to play tennis. I used to have self-esteem. One particular evening, I played pickleball with my husband. In my defense he had been playing with a group of people three times a week for several months. And unlike me, he doesn't look like a pickle.

We played one on one. I haven't moved that much since I had 5 kids with chickenpox at the same time. It was my idea to play "just one more game" and his idea to laugh. We played 5 games. It took about 15 minutes.

The next time we played a game I actually set a record on the pickleball court. I did. Four games, four losses – in other words, I got pickled four times in a twenty-five-minute period. More times than a *Vlasic* cucumber. While he was playing pickleball, I was single-handedly ridding the area of mosquitoes. Now, I did get in some major hits in the process, but with his toothy super-hero grin he would hit it back to me to an area only *Flash* could get to in time.

So, what is the moral of the story? My husband and I do not have the same talents. He is competitive. I am not. He is outgoing. I am not. I may not be as good at pickleball, but he doesn't have the inclination or desire to write a book. His ministry to others is service. My ministry to others is prayer and giving. We are both members of the body of Christ but we each have a different function.

Some may have a gift of speaking from a pulpit. Some may have a gift of taking care of children during Sunday School. What good does it do to envy a person who has a different gift than you do? Neither the speaker nor the nursery worker is greater than the other. We are all members of the body of Christ, no matter what part we play. If we all work together to serve in the areas we triumph in, then the body of Christ will not only flourish but will also work like a well-oiled machine.

And how do we accomplish this? By not trying to be someone else. By rejoicing in the uniqueness God has placed in each of us. And by offering our gifts and desires to our Creator and trusting Him to fulfill His will in us.

Isaiah 64:8 (NAS) "But now, O Lord You are our Father, we are the clay, and You are our potter; And all of us are the work of Your hands."

14

Job 12:12 (NIV) "Is not wisdom found among the aged? Does not long-life bring understanding?"

One can only hope!

You know you belong in an adult community when:

1. You stretch your arm above your head and get slapped in the face with loose skin.

2. When the doctor's assistant insists that you are 5'2 1/2" when your high school P.E. record clearly states 5'4".

3. When you remember why you went into the kitchen when you are back in the bedroom.

4. When your chest is no longer seated in the upright position.

5. When a bird of prey circles above your head and you pinch yourself to make sure you are alive.

6. When you can fall asleep in the middle of the day while the shoot-out at the OK Corral is blasting on the TV in front of you.

7. When knee-high compression socks are part of your current fashion statement.

8. When you have a compulsion to purchase lawn ornaments, Mexican pottery, and metal cacti.

9. When your back is hunched over – not from osteoporosis – but from your pickleball stance.

10. When you bought a golf cart for the sole purpose of transporting your swim noodle, your teacup poodle, or your schnauzer-doodle.

11. When you are over the age of accountability. Way over.

I make fun of the aging process because for one thing, I cannot change a thing, so why not enjoy it, and even laugh about it. (It beats falling on my face and crying, that's for sure!) As I look over my life, with its joys, sorrows, accomplishments, and failures, I want nothing less than to say I have reaped something of value. Job's question is right on the mark. Shouldn't living all those years have produced wisdom?

The book of Proverbs is full of scriptures that speak of wisdom's value.

Proverbs 3:13-14 (NAS) "How blessed is the man who finds wisdom, and the man who gains understanding. For its profit is better than the profit of silver and its gain than fine gold."

Proverbs 8:11 (NAS) "For wisdom is better than jewels; and all desirable things cannot compare with her."

By the time you are old enough to live in an adult community, one can only hope that you have become wise in your old age. I have to say that in my sixties I definitely have learned a thing or two about choices, whether they are wise or not. And as a mother and grandmother I feel it is my duty to share what I have learned with those I love. That is, if my children or grandchildren care to listen.

Wisdom definitely can come with aging. Wisdom is not only attained by all the bumps in the road that you may have tripped over in life or by the pain and sorrow that you experienced because of your own bad choices. Wisdom is a free gift from God. He offers it to every believer. One must only be willing to seek it.

James 1:5 (NAS) "But if any of you lacks wisdom, let him ask of God, who gives to all men generously and without reproach, and it will be given to him."

15

Proverbs 13:12a (NAS) "Hope deferred makes the heart sick."

I need a doctor, STAT!

Hope is realized when you least expect it, and this was definitely a dream come true.

It had been six weeks into the pandemic when everything began to look gray and dingy. And I am not just talking about my hair color. However, looking like a skunk can really get a girl down.

Every newscaster on every channel on the television, radio, and internet was telling me to stay home as much as humanly possible, avoid contact with others, and always wear a face mask. However, the only message I heard out of all of their ramblings was: you cannot get your hair done.

Say what?

I was allowed to go to Walmart and Fry's amid every form of human on the planet, wrestle another senior on the germ-covered floor over the last roll of toilet paper, but I was forbidden to get my hair done? I could blindly order a quarter pounder with cheese and a small fry at McDonalds without any assurance that none of it was seasoned with the newest and most deadly virus. But I was destined to wear a ballcap for the rest of my life?

"Travesty! Socialism! Communism!" my inner extrovert screamed.

I was definitely having a melt-down.

My sister, who owns a hair salon in Peoria, was forced to close her doors for the unforeseeable future. My daughter, also a hairdresser, was not allowed to enter her shop as well. I was forbidden by both of them to use an over-the-counter hair coloring product with the warning that the combination of chemicals already on my head might cause my hair to burst into flames. And since red is not my color, I obeyed.

Face masks were great at covering up anything undesirable on my face, like the lack of makeup or chapped lips, but it did nothing for the stark white highway that traveled from one end of my head to the other. I know this sounds petty, and perhaps it was, but even the Bible says a woman's hair is her glory and my glory was dead and gone. I really needed a resurrection!

When I finally reached the point of ending it all, by what my sister and I call death by shopping cart, my daughter called and asked me to come over. We had all been healthy, except for seasonal allergies, and we were certain we were covid-19 free. When I arrived at her house, she surprised me with a salon chair placed strategically in her kitchen, chemicals ready in a bowl, and an overly zealous desire to beat my gray roots into submission.

And although it may sound vain to those who were blessed with a head full of thick luscious and beautiful white hair, to me, this was certainly a blessing.

Don't you love it when in the midst of our frustrations, God comes through with a little blessing that lets us know that He cares for even the little things in our lives?

Proverbs 13:12b (NAS) "But desire fulfilled is a tree of life."

16

Luke 2:10-11 (NAS) "And the angel said to them, "Do not be afraid; for behold, I bring you good news of great joy which shall be for all people; for today, in the city of David there has been born for you a Savior, who is Christ the Lord."

No sweeter words!

Taking a stroll around my neighborhood during the Yuletide season is a stark reminder that a Christmas Hallmark movie will never be filmed here. For one reason, there will never be enough snowfall to produce one snowball. And there is ALWAYS snow in Christmas Hallmark movies.

Fuzzy red and white Santa hats atop fake metal cacti, plastic icicle lights lining tire-streaked driveways, and seventy plus degree weather does not, for me, conjure up a desire to cuddle in front of a warming fire while sipping on a hot and spicy mug of apple cider.

However, we can all agree that Christmas is the most festive time of year. Even in my bah humbug state of mind, I can't deny the excitement that seems to electrify the air. The heady scent of cinnamon that hits you as you enter a store, the colorful and often shimmering light displays gracing houses everywhere, the gift exchange, and cookie baking, and the carols that one only hears but once a year definitely add to the magic.

Last year, on my early morning walk I couldn't help noticing a sad deflated Santa in a neighbor's front yard. I was instantly inspired to hurry home and write a poem for the poor fella. This is what I wrote:

Inflatable Santa

Inflatable Claus, I simply must pause and asked what happened to you.

On a day that is sunny, I'm wondering, Honey, why you're feeling so blue.

You are puffed up at night in a colorful light, jolly,
happy, alert.

When daylight arrives, it's quite a surprise to find you
passed out in the dirt.

I feel I must mention a slight intervention may possibly
be your next plight.

There is simply a chance, Sir, a reindeer named Prancer
spiked your eggnog last night.

© 2019 - M.B. Roosa

In my community there are many expressions of Christmas, but unfortunately few display the true meaning of the season. Shouldn't the good news of Jesus' arrival be shouted from our snowless rooftops? Shouldn't the birth of the King of Kings be our focus rather than a jolly ole' elf and his reindeer?

Now just to be clear, I don't believe anything is wrong with Christmas decorations or celebrating Santa Claus. Trust me, I have a list of my favorite Christmas movies that I watch every year. And I love when my family gets together around our tree and in a frantic explosion of Christmas paper and ribbon, they unwrap their gifts. If that's what it takes to bring family together in a few short moments of inexplicable joy and laughter, then so be it!

But my hope is that we never forget what we are truly celebrating. We must take time to stop for a moment during this busy and sometimes hectic season and in humble gratitude, thank the Lord for the greatest gift of all, His son Jesus. For without Him, there would be no joy.

Luke 2:14 (NAS) "Glory to God in the highest, and on earth peace among people with whom He is pleased."

17

Luke 2:9 (NAS) "And an angel of the Lord suddenly stood before them, and the glory of the Lord shone around them; and they were terribly frightened."

Lest we forget.

I love to make people laugh. I think it's important for everything I write to start out with something light and end on a positive note. But I have to admit that the end of 2020 has left me without much humor.

It was the day before Christmas, and I had seriously lost my funny. That was not good. It's Jesus and my sense of humor that has gotten me thus far. I still have Jesus, of course, but I truly needed to find something to laugh about.

Every Christmas I have a household of family members, eating, laughing, chatting, opening gifts. It's a joyous occasion. We have seven kids, their spouses, and all our grandchildren. You can only imagine the chaos that occurs when the entire family gathers. Happy chaos. Even when they can't all make every holiday for whatever reason, there is always a lot of people in our home.

Except this particular year.

We had two families at Thanksgiving. It was still an enjoyable time (and quite frankly, a lot less work) although we all missed the rest of the clan. Due to Covid-19, Christmas was reduced to me and my husband. You have to understand, that we had never done Christmas alone. When we got married, we already had 6 children. A blended family. When one of our daughters, who was thankfully COVID-19-free, invited us for brunch. We were ecstatic.

Covid-19 stole so much from so many families in 2020. Loved ones died tragic deaths, businesses closed, income was lost, and fear itself caused people to decline gathering altogether. We were destined to don masks and gloves, drop Christmas gifts on doorsteps, ring doorbells, sprint, and dive through the window of our running car so that nobody would be exposed.

And yes, I did remember to roll down the window first.

My prayer as we ended the year was that our focus would be on the star of Bethlehem that points us to the manger where our hope of eternal life was born. No gift is greater. No sacrifice so powerful. No peace so palpable. No Savior but Jesus. He is the same yesterday, today, and forever.

Isaiah 9:6b (NAS) "And His name will be called Wonderful, Counselor, Mighty God, Eternal Father, Prince of Peace."

18

Nehemiah 8:10b (NIV) "Do not grieve, for the joy of the Lord is your strength."

I could use some of that joy about now!

Perhaps, it's because my blood type is B-negative. Perhaps, when I had a recent surgery, the doctor accidentally removed my funny bone as well. I don't know. But I feel the need to vent.

When Christmas has come and gone as it has every year before and all decorations and light displays have been removed from eaves and front yards and packed away in cardboard boxes for next year, my neighborhood is instantly transformed back to the same dull beige kingdom as before the colorful holiday. And I must admit it can be quite depressing.

I have lived in Arizona all my life minus three years and have never been impressed with the desert scenery. Dirt, sand, rock, cacti – eh. Boring. None of these inspire joy or good feelings within me. Even the tall Saguaros seem to be giving the world "the finger" and I really don't blame them. How would you like to stand out in the dirt, day after day, year after year, without a bit of shade or protection from haboobs, lightening, and summer's burning temperatures? Not I.

But I digress.

When Spring arrives with its reprieve from the drab dullness to an array of colorful wildflowers spread across the desert floor, it also brings for me a hint of hope. It's like the movie *Pleasantville* when color begins to slowly seep into the lives of their very gray world. That is something I truly look forward to.

This can also be a tiny example of what it is like to go through grief or depression. We all have experienced loss in our lives whether it's someone we love, a job, or the life we had envisioned for our future. It is during those moments when all we can do is lean in to the

One who not only gives us the strength to persevere, but also can give us joy in the midst of our sorrow.

So, for now, I will continue going for my daily strolls, try to ignore the rude Saguaros, and focus on the outlandishly colorful athletic clothing that the winter visitors so readily wear when swatting flies on the pickleball courts. And if that doesn't lift my spirit out of its current slump, I will look up to the sky where the bluest of blues brings my focus back to where it belongs and thank God that He is my source, my joy, and my hope.

Psalms 51:12 (NIV) "Restore to me the joy of Your salvation and grant me a willing spirit, to sustain me."

19

Job 1:21a (NAS) "Naked I came from my mother's womb, and naked I shall return there.

But please cover me up before the paramedics arrive!

Every new year that rolls around, us humans tend to make resolutions that we stick to for about a week and a half before finishing up all the Christmas cookies that we "hid" in the freezer for a special occasion. Unfortunately, for me, I discovered that I prefer frozen cookies over freshly baked ones. And so, goes another year of broken resolutions.

We can all agree that the year 2020 took a toll on all of us. The pandemic, division in our nation, election complications, loss of friends, loss of toilet paper and income put most of our new year's resolutions on hold. Because quite frankly, as we entered 2021, things did not appear any better.

As were most Christians I know, I was praying (basically crying out to God) to heal our nation. In fact, I couldn't help wondering if God was mad at us. I mean, why didn't He simply remove the pandemic from the world? Why wasn't He sending fire down from heaven to consume all those evil doers who were threatening our country's freedom? He did it in the Old Testament, didn't He? He was able, wasn't He? Am I the only one who wondered where God was in all of this?

And then I began to consider: Could it be possible that God was more concerned with what was taking place within each individual heart than what was happening in the world around us?

Job was the wealthiest man of his time. I guess you could say he was the Elon Musk of the Old Testament. His possessions were greater than anyone in the east. And the favor of God was obviously upon him. That is, until everything he knew and loved was suddenly stripped from him.

In one single day, he not only lost all of his oxen, donkeys, sheep, camels, and all of his servants except four of them, but he also lost all ten of his children. How devastating! Even if one of my children died, though I know they would be with Jesus, it would be the end of me. I cannot imagine bearing the loss that Job encountered. But despite all of it, what did Job do? Job shaved his head, tore his robe, and fell to the ground and worshipped. He worshipped!

Job lost everything and still he worshipped. I stub my toe on the nightstand in the middle of the night and the last thing on my mind is worship! In fact, there's a good chance that I may have to ask for forgiveness.

If that day for Job wasn't bad enough for one Godly man to bear, God allowed one more thing to happen. Job was struck with boils. This I can relate to. When I was in grade school I struggled with the development of seemingly endless boils on various parts of my body. They were extremely painful, impossible to get rid of, and quite embarrassing. When my mother took me to the doctor, he discovered that I had somehow developed a staph infection. For the next four weeks I had to undergo a series of uncomfortable injections.

Job was not so fortunate. There was no remedy for his pain. There was no medication that would clear up his infection. Even his own wife was no comfort to him. In fact, she told him to curse God and die.

What was Job's response to his suffering?

Job 2:10b (NAS) "Shall we indeed accept good from God and not accept adversity?"

Wow!

Thankfully, Job's story does not end there. God did not leave Job to die in his suffering. In Job chapter 42, the Bible says that the Lord blessed the latter days of Job more than his beginning. God restored to him more than he had lost. And Job saw four generations before dying at a ripe old age.

Oh, to have the heart of Job! To plead our case before the Lord of Lords while still remaining in an atmosphere of worship! We had nothing when we entered this world. We will leave the world with nothing, except for the hope of our salvation and an eternity with the Father God. Let us commit our hearts to trusting Him. Let our prayers of help be ever seasoned with thanksgiving to a God who loves us, who knows all, who has our lives in His hands. And God, please give us the faith to be able to proclaim, like Job:

Job 13:15a (NAS) "Though He slay me, I will hope in Him."

20

Proverb 12:10a "The righteous care for the needs of their animals."

And then some.

There is no lack of beasts in our community. And I'm not talking about the resident who demanded that my grandson remove himself from *her* spot in the *community* pool. I am referring to real, living, breathing animals that have been seen by some or most of the residents. Here is a partial list:

Owl, javelina, coyote, mountain lion, rattlesnake, cottontail, raccoon, silver fox (oh, wait, that's my husband), vulture, quail, cactus wren, and the list goes on. The recent drought and desert fires have caused many wild animals to flee the sparse and dry desert and roam our streets in search of their next meal. It's like a virtual zoo around here, except these animals are not tucked safely behind bars. Thankfully, I have only run into a few of them on my morning walks. And because it's chilly and I'm dressed like the Unabomber, they are evidently terrified of me.

Our HOA has strict warnings for those residents who leave food and water out for these unique beasts. However, I suspect some of the winter visitors who have never seen such a colossal species of creatures, do not pay attention to the rules. I mean, do they really want a mountain lion to crash their next barbecue? Not me. It is not as if these animals are going hungry. There is plenty of water on the golf course for birds and animals to drink and an abundance of vegetation and (unfortunately) bunnies to add to their grocery list.

But despite all of the above-mentioned critters in our neighborhood, family dogs reign supreme. For instance, some canines have their own personal chauffeurs. That is, those humans who take their puppies for a ride in their cherried-out convertible or waxed and polished golf cart for their daily bark fest or trip to the community dog park. Some have their own nannies. Those adults who pull a wagon or push a baby stroller carting their precious pooch in the name of "going for a walk".

You may be wondering where I am going with this, and believe it or not, I do have a point. Out of all the animals living and thriving in our community, not one of them is going without all they need to survive. Even the wild animals who wander our streets and avenues do not appear as if they have missed a meal.

If God cares about the needs of even the lowliest animal, how much more does He care about His people?

Matthew 6:26 (NAS) "Look at the birds of the air, that they do not sow, neither do they reap, nor gather into barns, yet your heavenly Father feeds them. Are you not worth much more than they?"

Do you ever worry about the future? I am not going to lie. I do sometimes. I see all the wickedness in the world and even in our country and I can't help feeling anxious about what it might mean for my children and grandchildren. And yet, I have to remind myself that God will never leave them nor forsake them. You don't have to search far to discover that there are so many other scriptures in the Bible that speak of God's love and care for us.

So, the next time you find yourself worrying about whether your needs will be met, whether there will be enough chicken noodle soup or toilet paper in your local grocery store, look at the chubby bulldog or decked out poodle in your neighborhood and allow it to remind you that if God cares for these critters, He certainly cares for you.

Psalms 37:25 (NAV) "I have been young, and now I am old; Yet I have not seen the righteous forsaken, or his descendants begging bread."

21

Psalms 23:4a (KJV) "Yea, though I walk through the valley of the shadow of death, I will fear no evil; for Thou art with me."

Such timely and comforting words.

A single rose, flattened, crusted, and brown, tucked inside an old familiar Bible bound tightly together with the rubber band I wore when my hair was long. The rediscovery of this precious gift is a memory of a love gone too soon that was once alive and joyful, and a stark reminder of how far I have come since then. How is it possible that I have traveled such a distance? Through the seasons of life, I have found myself in autumn. The leaves are fading, and life is changing colors before me. One day, like the single rose, I will be tucked away in winter memories. And as the snow melts and flowers begin to poke their heads through the softened loam, spring will arrive in glorious heavenly beauty, and so will I.

There is no greater wilderness to walk through than the grief of someone you love. I have had to say goodbye to more than my share of loved ones throughout the years and although God has restored me and blessed me abundantly above all I could ask or think, each and every one of those precious people can never be replaced. Only memories, although fading with time, can keep them alive.

I live in a community where hearing of the death of a neighbor is not uncommon. It is sad, and although neighbors and friends can gather around, offer meals, and condolences, grief is a wilderness path that only those left behind can walk. We can stand with them and even hold them up in prayer. But we can never truly feel their pain.

Life is fleeting. It's a vapor. I don't mean to sound melancholy, but none of us know the time when we are going to leave this temporal life and move on to the eternal. But one thing we can be sure of is where we will spend eternity. Do you believe in God? Do you believe He sent His son to die for us so that we can receive the forgiveness of sin? Do you believe He sent His Holy Spirit to bring us conviction and comfort? In other words, are you a "whosoever"?

John 3:16 (KJV) "For God so loved the world, that he gave His only begotten Son, that "whosoever" believeth in Him should not perish but have everlasting life."

In the seventies I was in a gospel band called Revelation. We traveled around and sang songs we wrote to glorify the Lord. I also sang duets with various friends and spent many hours in the middle of the night writing songs. Here is the chorus of a song I wrote during that time.

ONE DAY SOON

All our tears He'll wipe away.

All our nights He'll turn to day.

Singing and joy will fill the air.

Our sorrows here cannot compare,

to the glory we soon will share,

just because Jesus will be there.

© M.B. Roosa

There is such a comfort in knowing, not only where we are going after this life fades from view, but that with the presence of the Lord around us as we continue to walk this life, we have nothing to fear.

Psalms 91:4 (NAS) "He will cover you with His pinions, and under His wings you may seek refuge. His faithfulness is a shield and bulwark (defensive wall)."

22

Genesis 17:17 (NAS) "Then Abraham fell on
his face and laughed…"

*If what happened to Abraham's wife happened
to me, I'd be laughing all the way to the funny
farm!*

I am so grateful to the Lord for the gift of
writing. And I realize that even though I am not
in the same league as Joyce Meyer or Jentezen
Franklin, I still feel I have something to
contribute to the world. But even more than
writing, I love to make people laugh.

I inherited my sense of humor from my dad.
When I was a teenager and he was teaching me
how to drive he would say, "back up until you

hear glass." That still makes me crack up. And yes, I knew he was kidding. But his sense of humor was the very thing that helped me to relax while learning something that would otherwise have been stressful.

The one thing about living in an adult community is there seems to be endless comedic material to write about. Here is an example:

OUR COMMUNITY POOL

Our community pool is a place that is cool for everyone other than me.
I watch as they swim from my perch in the gym and here are some things I see.

There are skimmers and floaters, and certified loafers who love to nap in the sun.
There are volleyball lobbers, non-swimmers, and bobbers, wanting to simply have fun. I caught a glimmer of a passionate swimmer with flippers, goggles, and lotion.

She was swimming with zeal like a crabeater seal being chased by a shark in the ocean. With sunscreen and blocker, the stalkers and gawkers are looking for wife number three. The gal in bikini, who's slender and teeny, enjoys the attention you see. To my husband's chagrin, I will never jump in - quite frankly I'd rather be dead.
Seeing a grandpa in Speedo is the reason why I go to my daughter's pool instead.

© 2019 - M.B. Roosa

However, as much as I love to laugh there are times when laughter is not appropriate. And on that note, I have a confession to make and it's extremely embarrassing to admit. I haven't always obeyed this scripture. Have you ever been in a situation that was far from comical, and yet something hit your funny bone at the most inappropriate time and an involuntary giggle escaped your lips? Of course, this kind of thing isn't surprising when it happens to a kid. But what if you are an adult and at a funeral?

Yes. I am sorry to say. This happened to me. My husband and I entered the church. Except for the occasional clearing of the throat or sound of sniffing, the place was respectfully quiet. As it should be. Now normally the casket is positioned in the front of the sanctuary so that those who attend can focus on their loved one and say their final goodbyes. But not at this funeral. As we took our seats I leaned over to my husband and whispered, "where is she?" In which he replied, "she's sitting back there."

When I turned to see where they had placed the casket, I had to slap a hand across my mouth, because she was literally *sitting* back there. They had this sweet woman propped up in her casket in a semi-seated position, something I had never witnessed before in my life. Unfortunately, it hit my funny bone at the most inopportune time and a snicker welled up within me to which I had to stifle with a series of well-placed coughs. As you can imagine, I was mortified.

Life is full of so many sad things. It seems the older I get the less there is to laugh about. And yet, shouldn't the times of laughter in our lives outweigh the times of weeping? (Except, of course, at a funeral.) If we truly focus our attention on the God who loves us, who died so we could be saved, and who offers all good things to His children, won't the things of earth grow dim in the light of His goodness? Shouldn't the very thought of eternity with Jesus make us giddy? So, let us grasp hold of the joy He so willingly offers and give ourselves the freedom to laugh and laugh often.

Proverbs 17:22a (NAS) "A joyful heart is good medicine."

Nehemiah 8:10b (NKJV) "Do not sorrow, for the joy of the Lord is your strength."

Psalms 126:2 "Then our mouth was filled with laughter, and our tongue with singing. Then they said among the nations, The Lord has done great things for them."

23

Isaiah 46:4a (NAS) "Even to your old age I will be the same, and even to your graying years I will carry you!"

Lift with your legs, Lord. I'm holding water.

Old age is nothing to laugh about. But I can't help it. Because if I don't laugh, I may cry. And how encouraging would that be? Whether you want to hear this or not, one day you will be where I am, and I simply want you to be prepared.

No matter how many aerobic classes you attended during your child-bearing years, no matter how many steps you accumulated on your Fitbit, no matter how many salads you ate instead of burgers and fries, once you hit a certain age your body is different. It just is. Some parts even go on strike. And they refuse to return to work without some serious negotiating.

Here are a few things you may or may not experience in your senior years:

1. Your empty nest is so empty there is an echo.

2. The hair you once had on your head is now making an appearance on your chin.

3. Your twin peaks look more like a mudslide.

4. You have tendinitis, a bum knee, or need shoulder surgery.

5. You have a different doctor for every part of your body.

6. Your fallen arches have caused your feet to go so flat you could play Fred Flintstone in the next Hanna-Barbera movie.

7. You have so many spider veins you need to call for pest control.

8. Your six-pack has turned into a beer keg.

Of course, you could spend your entire

401K on cosmetic surgery to fix a lot of the damage done by all the years of fighting gravity. But most of us would rather use that money for things we could never purchase when our kids needed braces, or private school tuition - like adult braces and going-back-to-college tuition.

When you are young and look to the future, you discover that you have a lot of living to do. You are not concerned about where your kids may put you when you are too old to live on your own. You are not even considering the wrestling match that will ensue when they try to take your car keys away from you. You don't think about Social Security or Medicare. Your mind is on school, career, family, ministry, and enjoying the life before you.

As I find myself closer to the end of days, I feel motivated to make the last years of my life even more valuable than my former years - if at all possible. What legacy can I leave my children and my children's children? How many scriptures can I memorize so I will always have them ready when life becomes difficult? How can my life bring the most glory to the One who has not only saved me but who has walked with me through every season of life? Of course, all of these are things you can begin to do at any age.

On the day that the Lord finally calls me home, with every fiber of my being I want to be able to proclaim with confidence these words:

Philippians 1:21 "For to me, to live is Christ, and to die is gain."

24

Proverbs 27:20 (KJV) "Hell and destruction are
never full; so, the eyes of man are never
satisfied."

Preach it, sister!

Living in an adult community is different than
a regular neighborhood because the majority of
all the residents happen to be my peers. Of
course, there are some younger and those quite
a few years older, but for the most part we are
pretty much all in the same age category.
Because of that, I occasionally find myself a bit
envious of the women playing tennis in short
skirts or shorts and wonder how it is possible
that they still have nice enough legs to pull it
off.

I'm not speaking of those few who have

spent so much money on cosmetic enhancement that they could have fed an entire village in a third world country. In those particular cases, the other man's grass is greener only because it's artificial turf.

Why, as humans, are we never satisfied? Those without children, whether by choice or health reasons, wish they had children. Those who have children wish they could get a break from their children. Those with natural curly hair wish their hair were straight. Women with straight hair wish their hair were curly. I simply wish I had as much hair on my head as I did when I was in my twenties.

I do have natural curly hair and I don't mind it so much now since there are new hair products available that help to tame my wild mane. But when I was in high school in the early seventies ALL the girls in my school had long shiny straight hair parted down the middle. I lived in a house with a swamp cooler – you know, the kind of air conditioner that only worked part of the Arizona summer and required water in order to blow semi-cold air. No matter how many tin-can-sized rollers I put in my hair, or how many times I ironed my hair with my mother's twenty-year-old iron, as soon as the humidity hit, the curls were back. Trust me, it was a Jesus-freak-hippy-girl's worst nightmare.

Isn't it a waste of valuable time to spend our lives focusing on things we cannot change? If we are going to long for something better in our lives, shouldn't it be something eternal?

This isn't heaven. I often have to remind myself of this. When I finally lay down my earthly body and step into the eternal, will I care whether or not I had to wear capris instead of shorts or tennis skirts? Will it matter whether or not the veins on my leg looked like a map to nowhere? When I finally see my reward seated upon His throne, won't the things of earth that seem so important now, fade from view in the light of His glory and grace?

Lord, help us to focus on the eternal while we are still on earth. Perhaps then we will realize that our satisfaction can only be met in You. And help us to not only be content in this life, but also thankful for all You have in store for us.

Philippians 4:11 (NKJV) "Not that I speak in regard to need, for I have learned in whatever state I am, to be content."

How can we accomplish this?

Philippians 4:13 (NKJV) "I can do all things through Christ who strengthens me."

25

Proverbs 31:15 (NAS) "And she rises while it is still night and gives food to her household, and portions to her attendants."

But what if she's retired?

I have never been a "morning person". Except, of course, when I was working and had to get up in order to get there early enough to ready myself for the day. Or when I was forced to be a mom and get my kids up for school. But even then, it took me a least an hour and an IV of caffeine to truly wake up.

There are people in our neighborhood who go to bed before the sun sets and then get up the next morning before the sun rises. Kudos for those people! I will never be one of them. As it is now, it takes me about an hour and twenty games of Spider Solitaire to go to sleep at night and a lot of stretching, moaning, and groaning in order to leave the bed in the morning.

But because my life belongs to Jesus, I want each morning that I awake to be a time to focus on His will for my life. What do you have for me today, Lord? What can I do for you and others today? Please help my attitude, Lord, because I would rather not do today.

Here is a poem I wrote awhile back that reflects these thoughts.

MY LIFE BELONGS TO JESUS

My life belongs to Jesus. His desires are my own.

Though life is quickly passing by, He leaves me not alone.

What to do for him today? Each morning is my cry.

Love yourself and one another is His quick reply.

My life belongs to Jesus. He's my joy, my hope, my all.

Today again I'll walk with Him and listen for His call.

© 2019 - M.B. Roosa

Do you ever have mornings when you don't want to wake up? Do you ever feel like you don't have enough energy or desire to face another day? Do you ever want to toss a pillow at the window when the sun breaks through the mini-blinds and hits you square in the face? It can be a real battle.

As we awake and face another day, God is there in the wee morning hours waiting for us to come to Him, to spend time with Him, and to seek His will for our day. He is faithful to meet us where we are (even when we wake up a little grumpy). For this "night owl", that is worth all the stretching, moaning, and groaning it takes to get me up in the morning.

Lamentations 3:22-23 (NAS) "The Lord's acts of mercy indeed do not end, for His compassions do not fail. They are new every morning; Great is Your faithfulness."

26

Psalms 91:10 (NAS) "No evil will befall you, nor will any plague come near your tent."

Good news to hang onto during a pandemic.

During the spring of the pandemic, I had a difficult time writing. So instead of sitting at my laptop and staring at a blank page, I walked, I baked, I cooked, I ate, and well, I stocked up on toilet paper when it was available.

While my husband was keeping himself busy by creating things and building things (like his biceps), he was also faithfully laying out in the sun every day to absorb his dose of vitamin D and turning his skin to a healthy bronze tone. So, after teasing him relentlessly of looking like George Hamilton, he took one look at my ghostly white legs and changed my name – which finally sparked a bit of writing inspiration.

NAME CHANGE

I live in a ghost town where saguaros are tall,

And cottontails hide when coyotes call.

Yet I don't wear a holster and I do not drink beer.

So, when I ride into town, there is nothing to fear.

I don't smoke cigars and I don't own a horse.

Never been in an Eastwood movie of course.

But since my husband is tan now, and I am much whiter,

He changed my name today to "Pale Writer."

© 2020 - M.B. Roosa

As of this writing, the pandemic is not yet over, but so far, my husband and I have dodged the virus by the skin of our teeth and have received both of our vaccines. I seriously owe it all to God's grace and mercy, and Psalms 91 to which I claim daily over our family. Many in our neighborhood were not so fortunate. And the sadness that many families have had to endure during this pandemic is heartbreaking. I cannot remember another season in my lifetime that something has had such a horrible effect on every human on the planet.

One would think, that since all of us are going through this season together, that it would form some kind of unity among humanity. But unfortunately, it seems the worst has come out of many people during this time and unity does not seem to be the case at all. The division, even among God's people, is a complete waste of what God could be teaching us here.

What's it going to take for all of us on earth to remember that we are ALL made in the image of God? Have you ever taken a good look at the stone called jasper? There is one in particular that contains every color of human flesh, from the darkest darks to the lightest lights. Did you know that God contains all these colors as well?

Revelations 4:2-3a (NKJ) "Immediately I was in the Spirit; and behold, a throne set in heaven, and One sat on the throne. And He who sat there was like a jasper…."

What an amazing revelation! God loves all of His people. Even me, with my pasty white legs. Shouldn't this be a lesson for us to let go of any division and rejoice in our differences. Because quite frankly, if we all truly give it some thought, we will find we have much more in common, than not.

2 Corinthians 13:11 (NAS) "Finally, brothers and sisters, rejoice, mend your ways, be comforted, be like-minded, live in peace; and the God of love and peace will be with you."

27

Deuteronomy 32:10 (NAS) "He found him in a desert land, and in the howling wasteland of a wilderness; he encircled him, He cared for him, He guarded him as the apple of His eye."

He is our only hope in the dry and desert wasteland.

Have you ever looked up the word "wilderness"? The dictionary states that it is an uncultivated, uninhabited, and inhospitable region. And quite frankly, I oftentimes feel like that is where I live. Especially in the summer when most of my neighborhoods are heading north to greener pastures.

Here is a poem I wrote while considering

my neighborhood and surrounding Arizona desert. (My apologies ahead of time.)

DESERT LIVING

I live in a desert where rattlesnakes roam.

Where my husband finds one and brings it home.

He kills it and skins it and watches it squirm.

Then seasons and barbecues the venomous worm.

I live in the desert where the dust in the air,

Makes itself home on my floor and my hair.

Where palo verde pollen moves on a breeze,

Like soft yellow snowflakes, that's making me sneeze.

I live in the desert where summer is cruel.

Where dressing appropriately isn't a rule.

Where Grannies in shorts and Grandpas in speedo

Do nothing for Grannie's and Grandpa's libido.

I live in the desert. God only knows why,

I'd prefer a cabin on a mountain so high.

Or a beach house or cottage, down by the sea.

But I doubt my husband would go there with me.

I live in the desert where cacti are trees,

Where blossoms are pollinated by African bees.

I live in the desert where the temperatures swell,

Which makes me grateful I'm not going to hell.

I walk with a neighbor several times a week and the amazing thing about her is that while I am mentally poo-pooing all the desert landscaped yards we pass by and dull dirt-colored houses, she will spot a cactus flower a mile away, stop, and get entranced by its beauty. My friend is from Minnesota and she is enthralled with the desert foliage. And if I didn't walk with her during the spring months, I would never take notice of some of the most magnificent flowers that God has placed in the desert to demonstrate the glory of His creation.

Wilderness can mean so many different things to so many people. It is not only a physical location, but it can also be a spiritual or emotional place. Out of curiosity I have asked family members and friends "what does wilderness mean to them?" And everyone had a story about a trial or tribulation they passed through at some point in their life.

The amazing thing of walking with God through the wildernesses of life is that even when things seem dark around us, we can rest in the assurance that He is there to encircle us, to care for us, and to guard us as the apple of His eye. The character of our God becomes the most obvious when we take time out of our busy schedules to admire the beauty of His creation.

Romans 1:20 (NAS) "For since the creation of the world His invisible attributes, His eternal power and divine nature, have been clearly seen, being understood through what has been made, so that they are without excuse."

28

Romans 8:18 (NAS) "For I consider that the sufferings of this present time are not worthy to be compared with the glory that is to be revealed to us."

I don't know about you, but I cannot wait!

Another ominous and blistering summer day. As I walk, the sun stings my cheeks, and a hot wind whips my hair around my face. I see an American flag in a neighbor's yard twisted around a rocking pole. I glance up to an eerie sky. Thin clouds are like ghosts streaking across the blue. Perhaps, they are being pursued by angels.

One can only hope.

Streets are as empty as a tax collector's heart. I half expect to see the coyote which frequents our neighborhood in search of its next meal. His eyes frantically search for substance. Your heart wants to leave him a scrap of meat. But your mind knows that you cannot.

He will only be back for more.

As I return home, I immediately realize that this story must be told. Because going to get the mail would be so boring if I didn't have something to write about.

Being a writer is a lot of work. Even when inspiration presents itself wrapped in a fancy box with a ribbon. Writers have to write. We do. It's in our very nature to sit in front of our laptop or pad of paper and let our heart bleed ink. But writing something that not only makes people chuckle yet is also meaningful and points them to the Creator is the reason that I write.

Reverend Bob Mumford put it this way: "Make them smile then hit them in the teeth." I love that!

There will always be times in our lives where nothing makes us laugh. Where our hearts have been so wounded that it's difficult to even face another sunrise let alone find something to smile about. But if we truly consider the fact that this life, with all its trials and tribulations, is only a tiny fraction of the eternal life that awaits us, we can at the very least find joy to celebrate what awaits us in heaven.

I have a confession to make. As I was working on this book, I began to feel like perhaps there was nothing worthy in what I was writing. I mean, how could someone like me, with a rather bizarre sense of humor, minister to anyone? To be honest, I always struggle with the fact that I am not a pastor or a Bible scholar.

One day, during my personal pity party, I heard the Lord's still small voice whisper to me. He said, "I did not call you to change the whole world. I called you to be you."

Talk about freedom! Talk about the lifting of the heavy burden I felt every time I sat down to write! So, if anything I share regarding what I have learned from a lifetime of walking with Jesus, studying his word, and listening to those who are called to change the world, ministers to even one person, I will be content. Because when it all comes down, it is not about me. It is about Jesus. Because only He, and He alone can change our world.

John 16:33 (NAS) "These things I have spoken to you, that in Me you may have peace. In the world you have tribulation, but take courage, I have overcome the world."

29

Psalms 55:6 (NKJV) "So I said, "Oh that I had wings like a dove! I would fly away and be at rest."

However, not the species of dove that fly in front of my windshield on the freeway.

I thought it was a bat. It flew like a bat. It dipped and soared erratically like a bat. I was returning home from getting my mail when it flew out from the entryway to my front door and scared the bejeebies out of me. Trust me. I have no bejeebies left.

It was larger than a dove or a sparrow or even a pigeon. It flew on stiff black wings that moved up and down in unison. And even when it left my entryway, it was not startled away to the nearest roof. It made a noise like no bird I'd ever heard before, except perhaps on *JURASSIC PARK*, (a pterodactyl, if you will) and kept flying around the same area, swooping, and diving, much like a bat.

So, of course, I got out my cell phone and looked up birds in Arizona that act like bats and this is what I discovered. The bird is called The Lesser Nighthawk. I'd hate to see what the Greater Nighthawk looks like. All I know is that it's the same species of bird that almost knocked a friend of mine off of her bicycle.

When I was a kid, I often had dreams that I was flying. Of course, right before crashing to the ground, I woke up. Thank the Lord! I have no idea what that meant, all I know is that the feeling of flying was exhilarating, and I didn't want it to end.

Do you ever feel like flying away? Do you ever feel like the things going on in the world today only cause your desire to go to heaven much more palpable? Do you ever wish the Lord would return and take His people from all the lawlessness and evil of this world? Well, I do. Quite frankly, I can't watch the evening news anymore or I would never get any rest.

But what is required of us while waiting for

the time when the Lord calls us to fly away home? Oftentimes, we are left here to grieve friends and loved ones who have crossed over to the eternal, and we wonder why they were chosen to go before us. My kids hate it when I speak of going home to be with the Lord. (On one hand, it's nice to know they'd miss me) Yet, as much as I love them and want to be used by the Lord to pray for them and serve them as long as I am able, I have, perhaps, a unique view of heaven. It became quite real to me at the age of thirty when I lost my first husband, Jack.

When I was ushered into the cold and sterile hospital room to say goodbye, and I saw my sweet husband's "empty shell" lying there, the Lord revealed heaven to me like a beautiful revelation. We all know that when we give our lives to the Lord, He gives us eternal life. That means that although our body dies, our spirits are still very much alive. So, when we "fly away", so to speak, it's our spirits who go home to be with the Lord. Our bodies are part of us, for sure. But they are only the vessel that contains who we really are inside. And some day, we will also receive a glorified body. I am so looking forward to a body without flat feet!

So, although we must wait for the beautiful moment when we see Jesus, face to face, let us not grow weary in our faith. Let us keep pressing on to walk out this life in which He has called us. Let us give all that we have until there is no longer a breath in our lungs. Then, on our appointed time, we will indeed fly away and be at rest.

2 Corinthians 5:8 (NAS) "But we are of good courage and prefer rather to be absent from the body and to be at home with the Lord."

30

Psalms 139:16 (NAS) "Your eyes have seen my formless substance; And in Your book were written all the days that were ordained for me, when as yet there was not one of them."

After having five kids, I look like a formless substance.

A tiny wing of a Monarch butterfly lay on our gray concrete driveway - a remnant of a beautiful life, now gone forever. I was captivated by the beauty of God's creation, delicately painted in orange, black, and yellow. I hurried for my phone so I could take a picture. But alas, I returned only to find that the wind had whipped the colorful remnant off to a new location. And I pondered how if only my life so transient, so fleeting, could leave a tiny touch of God's beauty behind as the wind whipped my soul to eternity, it would be enough.

When you get to be my age, you can't help but wonder how much time you have left on earth. When I was in my twenties, the thought never came to mind. I had an entire lifetime ahead. Or so I imagined. But the moment when you start receiving your social security check, you know things are about to get serious.

I know I speak about life, death, and eternity often in this book. But the fact remains, no matter what age we are we still can only count on today. My brother passed away when he was nine years old. How can it be that God granted him such a short life when he had so much time ahead of him? His death had a profound impact on my parents and our family. His short life even had a lasting effect on some of his young friends. Our earthly minds cannot begin to understand the mind of God. But it is God's promise to us that one day, it will all make sense.

The Bible says in 1 Corinthians 13:12 (NAS) "For now we see in a mirror dimly, but then face to face; now I know in part, but then I will know fully, just as I also have been fully known."

In the meantime, how shall we then live? Should we give up and hang onto the past so hard we cannot move forward? Should we lay our past, no matter what it is, at the feet of the cross and trust God for today, tomorrow, and forever? It's not that we will ever forget the loss or pain we have endured or those who have gone before us. But it is putting all of our trust in a God who knows all and has our lives in His hands.

Life is fleeting. It rides the waves of elation and sadness, of anger and calm, of harmony and discord until it rolls onto the shore where our souls will finally find rest. No matter what we go through, He promised He would always be there to walk with us, to hold us, to care for us. Christ defeated death when He gave Himself up on the cross, so in reality we who love the Lord are already in eternity.

In the meantime, how can we in this life that is oftentimes full of pain and sorrow find true joy? The joy is in the salvation He has so freely granted.

1 Peter 1:8-9 (NAS) "And though you have not seen Him, you love Him, and though you do not see Him now, but believe in Him, you greatly rejoice with joy inexpressible and full of glory, obtaining as the outcome of your faith the salvation of your souls."

31

Job 8:21 (NAS) "He will yet fill your mouth
with laughter and your lips with shouting."

Laughter is indeed good medicine.

Living in an adult community has
accomplished two things for me. First of all, it
has given me a reality check about how old I
really am. Thank you very much! And second
of all, it has given me a reason to laugh because
of it.

Have you ever met anyone who had no
sense of humor? You crack a joke, and their
only reaction is a furrowed brow? I do not
understand people like that. Joy and laughter
are the only things that get me through this life.

If I stop laughing, call the morgue. This girl's spirit is on the way to Jesus.

I have a granddaughter who as of this writing is seven years old and she is hilarious. The best thing about it, is she doesn't even realize how funny she is until everyone starts laughing. Here are some examples of the things she has said over the years.

- Me to Eva: "Do you have something stuck in your tooth?" Eva: "Yes. I need a tooth pickle."

- Eva pulling a dart gun out of her toy box. Eva: "I have a gun. A son of a gun."

- Eva: "I forgot to brush my hair." Me: "Do you want to brush it now?" Eva: "Not today, Junior."

- Eva: "Nana, remember when you were taller than heaven sakes alive? And now you're shrinking?"

- Eva: "There is sauce on the quesadilla." Me: "I told them no sauce." Eva: "It's probably because you are old, and they couldn't hear you."

- My personal favorite - Eva: "Nana. Dance like you have one leg."

I cannot imagine going through this life without laughing. My sisters and I have been known to laugh so hard and long that there is no sound in the room because we cannot breathe. Those are some of the best memories of my life.

God never promised us that our entire earthy life would be full of joy and laughter. He promised us that no matter what we went through that He would always be with us. But like with Job, he also promised us that one day our mouths would again be filled with laughter.

Can you even imagine the joy that is before us? Can you imagine being in a place where we are enveloped in the love and light of our Savior? No matter what wilderness we must walk through in this life, no matter what trials and tribulations face us, there is a joy in knowing that one day we will see Jesus and He will wipe away all our tears. So let us take time out of our busy schedules and rejoice in a Savior who not only conquered death, and defeated the enemy, but has also prepared a place for those of us who love Him.

Isaiah 25:8a (NAS) "He will swallow up death for all time, and the Lord God will wipe tears away from all faces."

ACKNOWLEDGEMENTS

There are so many people I want to thank for inspiring me to write this book. However, if I missed your name, I apologize. I am old.

First and foremost, I give thanks to my Lord and Savior Jesus Christ for saving me and giving me a "voice" in the form of writing to share His love, joy, and mercy. Second, I want to thank my husband, Greg. There is no way I would have made this journey into Seniorville, without you.

I would also like to thank all of my *Facebook* friends and family who encouraged me to put my posts into book form. Thank you for the kick in the rear.

And, of course, I wouldn't have had the drive to leap over all the writer's blocks if it weren't for my sisters, my kids, and my grandchildren.

A special shout out to my granddaughter, Eva, for such great material to add to this book. You have no idea how often you make me laugh. Thank you to Corissa and Linda for catching the ridiculous typos this sixty-five-year-old brain skipped over. Thank you, James, ALWAYS for the amazing artwork and service you provide getting my work published. What would I do without you?

Thanks to my springtime walking buddy, Melane. Your blood type HAS to be B positive. It just does. Thank you, Mary, my amazing neighbor who is always just a text away even though we live across the street.

And last but not least, thank you Lord for introducing me to the amazing group of people in the community Writer's Table. You all have not only become my dear friends, but also an impelling encouragement that keeps this writer writing.

.

Made in the USA
Monee, IL
22 November 2021